WE LIKE TO HELP

HELPING

DOING, doing—I'm always doing!
And I think helping is fun!
Jesus wants me for a helper,
And He helps me to *be* one!

WASH DAY

I'm a wash day helper!
   See what I can do?
I can carry clothes for Mother,
   And help sort them, too!

Hummm and splish and splash!
   I like our washer's sound,
And it's fun when I can see
   The sudsy clothes go 'round!

Now our clothes are clean and dry
 And I can help by folding.
I put the towels where they belong;
 See the pile I'm holding!

Jesus wants me for a helper,
 And He helps me to *be* one!

CAR WASHING

Pails of sudsy water,
   Squishy sponges, too,
And some happy helpers
   Make our car look new!

Daddy soaps the top and windows,
   And I scrub each light,
Then I go sloshing round and round
   To make the hubcaps bright.

We hose the car on every side,
   We spray it up and down.
When we drive to church you'll see
   The cleanest car in town!

BROTHER'S BIRTHDAY

Today's my brother's birthday!
    We had so much to do.
I helped blow up some bright balloons,
    And set the table, too.

Colored streamers, funny hats,
    Nut cups and yummy candy,
Frilly favors to pop and toot,
    All made his party dandy.

But Brother likes his birthday cake
   Best of all, I know.
See, its shining candles tell
   How OLD God's helped him grow!

RESTING

Doing, doing—I'm always doing!
And I get tired—do you?
Resting is a way of helping,
For then Mommy can rest, too!

My eyes go wink,
My eyes go blink!
Pretty soon
They'll sleep I think...

Jesus wants me for a helper,
And He helps me to *be* one!

DUSTING

Mommy dusts the high-up things,
   While I dust the low;
It's hard for me to reach high up
   But I like bending, so —
You see, we help each other
   By doing what we can;
And soon our Daddy smiles and says,
   "This house looks spic and span!"

And our dear Heavenly Father
 Can see our clean house, too;
And I am sure that He is pleased
 That I have helped, aren't you?

SHOPPING

We are shopping helpers—
   See what we can do?
Brother likes to push the cart,
   Hold bags for Mommy too.

I like to try to find the things
   On my Mommy's list.
Sometimes I have to run back fast
   For things that Mom has missed!

Because we're shopping helpers,
   We don't whine and tease,
Helpers know that Mom can't buy
   Everything we please!

Jesus wants me for a helper,
And He helps me to *be* one!

A HELPING TOY

I sat alone on a see-saw board;
    It wasn't any fun at all
Till someone sat at the other end—
    Then up I went, so tall!

'Twas kind of scary up so high;
    I thought that I might fall,
But when my playmate smiled at me,
    I wasn't scared at all!

Down, down, down he helped me go.
    "Don't get off!" he said;
"If you do, please tell me quick
    Or I'll fall on my head!"

Up and down and up and down!
 Taking turns, each one,
When one is up, the other's down;
 A see-saw's lots of fun!

Jesus wants me for a helper,
And He helps me to *be* one!

THE TABLEWARE FAMILY

Knives are tall like daddies are,
    And the forks are more like mothers;
And I pretend the little spoons
    Are the sisters and the brothers.

I put a "family" by each plate—
    A knife, a fork, and spoon—
And when I give them "people" names,
    I finish very soon!

My mommy smiles, and I do too;
  Helping's so much fun!
When we make a game of it,
  Pretty soon it's done!

Our table's such a happy place,
  For first we bow to pray
And thank the Lord for giving us
  Such good food every day.

Jesus wants me for a helper,
And He helps me to *be* one!

DOING DISHES

I always wipe my face before
   I get up from the table;
But dishes cannot clean themselves,
   They really are not able.

And so my mommy washes them,
   And I help dry the small ones;
Some day I'll do them all myself,
   Even all those tall ones!